DOG FOOD COOKBOOK FOR FOOD ALLERGIES

Nova Winters

Copyright © 2023 by Nova Winters

All rights reserved. No part of this publication may be reproduced, stored in a retrieval system, or transmitted, in any form or by any means, electronic, mechanical, photocopying, recording, or otherwise, without the prior written permission of the publisher, except for brief quotations in critical reviews or articles.

Disclaimer:

The information provided in this book is intended for general informational purposes only. The author and publisher of this book are not responsible for any actions taken based on the content presented herein.

While every effort has been made to ensure the accuracy and completeness of the information provided, the author and publisher make no representations or warranties of any kind, express or implied, about the reliability, suitability, or availability of the content contained within this book.

Other Titles by The Author

INSTANT POT DOG FOOD RECIPES COOKBOOK

SLOW COOKER DOG FOOD COOKBOOK

KIDNEY DISEASE DOG FOOD COOKBOOK

HOMEMADE RECIPES COOKBOOK FOR SMALL DOGS

To check out ALL TITLES by the Nova Winters,

Click here or scan the QR code below

TABLE OF CONTENTS

INTRODUCTION 1

CHAPTER 1 7

Getting Started 7

    Understanding Food Allergies in Dogs 7

    Why Homemade Dog Food? 8

    How to Use This Cookbook 8

    Tips for Preparing Allergy-Friendly Meals 9

CHAPTER 2 11

Common Food Allergens in Dogs 11

    Identifying Common Allergens 11

    Allergic Reactions in Dogs 12

    Importance of Allergen-Free Dog Food 13

CHAPTER 3 15

Cooking Basics 15

    Essential Ingredients and Tools 15

Safe Food Handling for Dogs 16

Transitioning to Homemade Food 17

CHAPTER 4 19

Allergy-Friendly Ingredients 19

Proteins: Choosing the Right Meat 19

Carbohydrate Options 20

Healthy Fats and Oils 20

Fruits and Vegetables 21

Herbs and Supplements for Allergy Relief 21

CHAPTER 5 23

Breakfast and Brunch Recipes 23

Homemade Breakfast Bowls 23

Omelets and Scrambles 27

Nutritious Pancakes and Waffles 31

CHAPTER 6 35

Lunch and Dinner Delights 35

Protein-Packed Entrees 35

Grain-Free Side Dishes 39

Vegetable-Centric Meals 43

CHAPTER 7 47

Tasty Treats and Snacks 47

Allergy-Friendly Biscuits 47

Chewy and Crunchy Snacks 52

Frozen Treats for Hot Days 56

CHAPTER 8 61

Special Occasion and Celebration Meals 61

Birthday Cakes and Pupcakes 61

Holiday Feasts for Dogs 67

14-DAY MEAL PLAN 71

Week 1 71

Week 2 73

CONCLUSION 75

BONUS: Homemade Allergy Test Guides. 77

Guide 1: At-Home Allergy Test 77

Guide 2: Food Trial Template 79

INTRODUCTION

In a world filled with uncertainty and chaos, there exists a sanctuary of unwavering love and boundless loyalty—a sanctuary where wagging tails and soulful eyes fill our lives with immeasurable joy and unwavering companionship. That sanctuary is the realm of our beloved canine friends. These four-legged miracles, with their uncanny ability to turn our darkest days into beacons of light, have a unique place in our hearts. Yet, within the realm of love and companionship, there often hides a silent tormentor: food allergies.

Let me transport you to a moment of revelation, one that marked the genesis of the journey that brought this cookbook to life—a journey born of necessity and fueled by unwavering determination.

It was a crisp autumn day, and the air was filled with the rustling of leaves and the distant echoes of children's laughter. But for Brenda, a devoted dog parent, that day bore a heavy burden of worry and helplessness. Her voice trembled as she recounted the harrowing journey of her beloved companion, Max, a majestic Golden Retriever. Max had once been the embodiment of vitality, with a gleaming coat and an infectious zest for life. But over time, an insidious force had begun to unravel his health—the relentless grip of food allergies.

Brenda and her family had embarked on a relentless quest for answers, one that led them through the labyrinth of commercial dog foods, specialty diets, and ultimately, to a cookbook that promised a panacea for Max's troubles. Hope hung in the air as they ventured into this culinary journey, believing that the recipes within its pages would be the remedy they sought.

Yet, with each meal they prepared and each bite Max took, the promise of relief remained unfulfilled. The recipes, despite their enticing allure, proved to be ineffective. Max's suffering persisted, his itching and discomfort intensifying, and the once-shiny coat dulled into a shadow of its former glory.

Brenda's voice quivered with emotion as she recalled those heart-wrenching moments spent watching her beloved Max's condition deteriorate. "We were lost," she confessed. "Desperation had us in its grip, and we couldn't bear to see Max suffer any longer. We needed help, and we didn't know where to turn."

It was at this juncture, where despair met determination, that Brenda and Max's journey crossed paths with mine—a veterinarian nutritionist with a fervent passion for healing through the power of nutrition. Brenda's phone call was a lifeline, a plea for guidance, and a summons to action. With a heavy heart, Brenda and Max embarked on a journey to my clinic, where our paths would converge and destiny would unveil its plans.

The first meeting was a somber affair. As Max's weary eyes met mine for the first time, I could see the toll that allergies had taken on him. His once-lustrous coat was marred by patchy bald spots, his skin inflamed and irritable, and his once-joyous spirit dimmed by the relentless itch.

Our conversation was an emotional rollercoaster, filled with frustration, hope, and ultimately, determination. Brenda recounted their painful journey, detailing their investment in a popular dog food cookbook that had promised salvation but had failed to deliver. Max's condition, it seemed, had reached a point of no return.

As I listened to Brenda's desperate plea, a deep sense of responsibility washed over me. I realized that it was time to channel my expertise as a veterinarian nutritionist into guiding Max and Brenda toward a solution. The weight of their hope rested on my shoulders, and it was a burden I was willing to bear.

With a shared determination to heal Max and countless other dogs like him, Brenda and I embarked on a voyage of discovery. We delved into the intricate world of canine nutrition, studying, researching, and experimenting with a myriad of ingredients, all with the singular goal of finding a solution that would cater to Max's specific allergies while nourishing his body and soul.

Weeks turned into months, and we forged ahead, conducting meticulous trials and embracing every challenge with unwavering perseverance. We scoured scientific literature, consulted fellow veterinarians, and toiled endlessly to create a tailored, allergy-friendly diet that would transform Max's life.

And then, the breakthrough arrived. Max's skin began to heal, his coat regained its luster, and his boundless energy returned. It was a moment of pure magic, a testament to the incredible power of nutrition to heal and rejuvenate. The transformation was undeniable and utterly heartwarming.

One sunny morning, as Brenda and Max sat on my clinic's patio, Max's tail wagged furiously, radiating joy. Brenda looked at me with tears of gratitude glistening in her eyes. "You've given us our Max back," she whispered, her voice filled with emotion. "You've given us hope when we had almost lost it."

However, Max's story was not the end—it was merely the beginning. It was the birth of a mission, a mission to extend this newfound hope to countless other dogs and their families who were grappling with the torment of food allergies.

With the knowledge and recipes we had meticulously crafted, I embarked on the creation of this dog food cookbook. It wasn't just a cookbook; it was a testament to the resilience of the human-dog bond, a symbol of hope, and a source of healing. It was a treasure trove of meticulously crafted recipes, each designed with the utmost care to address the specific needs of dogs with food allergies.

As the pages of the cookbook came together, I knew that it was not just about providing nourishment; it was about offering a lifeline to dogs and their families who had endured the relentless trials of allergies. Each recipe within these pages was a gesture of love, a promise of relief, and a pathway to vibrant health.

The day we launched the cookbook was a momentous occasion, one filled with hope and excitement. It was as if we had cast a beacon of light into the world, illuminating the path to a healthier, happier life for countless dogs and their devoted families.

And the response was nothing short of miraculous. Success stories began to flood in, heartwarming tales of transformation and renewal that brought tears of joy to our eyes. Dog parents who had once felt the same desperation as Brenda and Max now rejoiced in the newfound vitality and well-being of their furry companions.

One letter, in particular, stands out in my memory. It was from a family in a small town, and their dog, Bella, had been plagued by allergies for years. They had journeyed through the labyrinth of commercial diets and had consulted multiple veterinarians, but Bella's relentless itching and discomfort had remained unchanged.

With a sense of trepidation, they had stumbled upon our cookbook, hesitant to place their faith in yet another promise of relief. But something in our journey, in the shared experience of countless others who had found success with our recipes, compelled them to give it a try.

They meticulously followed our recipes, sourcing the finest ingredients and preparing each meal with love and care. The first few weeks were filled with cautious optimism, as they monitored Bella's reactions, their hearts filled with the fragile hope of seeing her condition improve.

And then, it happened. Bella's itching began to subside, her coat regained its shine, and her energy levels surged. It was a transformation that brought tears to the eyes of Bella's family, a testament to the healing power of proper nutrition and care..

So, as you turn the page and delve into the world of allergy-friendly dog cuisine, know that you're not just reading a cookbook—you're joining a movement. A movement of compassion, understanding, and unwavering love for our four-legged companions. The journey begins here, and it's a journey of transformation, one meal at a time.

Welcome to the Dog Food Cookbook for Food Allergies—a labor of love, a testament to hope, and a source of healing for dogs and their devoted families. Your furry friend's journey to a healthier, happier life starts now.

CHAPTER 1
Getting Started

UNDERSTANDING FOOD ALLERGIES IN DOGS

Before we dive into the world of crafting delectable allergy-friendly meals for our furry companions, it's crucial to grasp the basics of food allergies in dogs. Just like us, our four-legged friends can develop allergies, and these allergies can manifest in various ways, from itchy skin to digestive issues. In this section, we'll unravel the mysteries of canine food allergies, helping you become a savvy chef for your pet.

Imagine your dog's immune system as a diligent gatekeeper. It's responsible for identifying and eliminating any potentially harmful substances that enter your dog's body. However, sometimes this vigilant system gets a bit too zealous and mistakes harmless ingredients in their food as threats, leading to an allergic reaction. These reactions can range from mild discomfort to severe distress, making it essential for us, as pet parents, to be mindful of what goes into their bowls.

By understanding the root causes and symptoms of food allergies in dogs, you'll be better equipped to provide your loyal companion with meals that not only nourish but also delight their taste buds.

WHY HOMEMADE DOG FOOD?

"Why should I bother making homemade dog food when commercial options are readily available?" you might wonder. It's a valid question, and one we'll address right here. While commercial dog foods offer convenience, they often contain a medley of ingredients that can trigger allergies in sensitive pups.

By preparing meals for your dog at home, you gain precise control over what ingredients go into their food bowl. You can tailor recipes to cater specifically to your dog's allergies, ensuring they receive a diet that keeps them happy, healthy, and allergy-free. Plus, there's something incredibly satisfying about whipping up a meal for your furry friend from scratch.

HOW TO USE THIS COOKBOOK

Now that you're convinced of the benefits of homemade dog food, let's discuss how to make the most of this cookbook. We've organized it to be user-friendly and informative. Each chapter will delve into a different aspect of crafting allergy-friendly meals for your dog, and the recipes included will cater to various dietary needs.

Feel free to explore the chapters in any order that suits your needs. If you're here because your dog has recently developed an allergy, you might want to jump straight to the recipe section. On the other hand, if you're new to the world of dog food allergies, we recommend reading through the chapters in order to gain a comprehensive understanding of the topic.

TIPS FOR PREPARING ALLERGY-FRIENDLY MEALS

Before you embark on your culinary adventure for your beloved pup, let's go over some essential tips for preparing allergy-friendly meals. These tips will help you navigate the kitchen with confidence, ensuring that every dish you create is not only safe but also irresistibly delicious for your dog.

1. Consult Your Vet: First and foremost, consult with your veterinarian to identify your dog's specific allergies. Knowing the allergens to avoid is key to creating safe meals.

2. Read Labels Carefully: When selecting ingredients, pay close attention to labels. Avoid any potential allergens, and opt for high-quality, hypoallergenic options when possible.

3. Keep It Simple: Simple recipes with a limited number of ingredients are often the safest choice for dogs with allergies. This reduces the chances of accidentally including an allergen.

4. Introduce New Ingredients Gradually: If you're trying out a new ingredient in your dog's diet, introduce it slowly and monitor for any adverse reactions.

5. Balance is Key: Ensure that your homemade meals provide a balanced diet, meeting your dog's nutritional needs. You may need to supplement certain nutrients, which we'll discuss in later chapters.

Now that we've set the stage, let's embark on this culinary journey together, dedicated to keeping our furry friends happy, healthy, and free from the discomfort of food allergies.

CHAPTER 2
Common Food Allergens in Dogs

IDENTIFYING COMMON ALLERGENS

Understanding the common food allergens for dogs is paramount when you're on a mission to create allergy-friendly meals. Just like with humans, dogs can be sensitive to a variety of ingredients that may trigger allergic reactions. In this chapter, we'll explore the most prevalent culprits when it comes to dog food allergies.

1. Grains: Wheat, corn, soy, and rice are some of the primary grains that can provoke allergies in dogs. These are often found in commercial dog foods, making them a frequent source of sensitivities.

2. Proteins: Certain proteins can be problematic for some dogs. Beef, chicken, and dairy are among the top offenders. It's important to note that while these proteins are common allergens, some dogs may be allergic to less typical sources like lamb or fish.

3. Dairy: Lactose intolerance is relatively common among dogs, which means dairy products like milk and cheese can lead to digestive discomfort.

4. Eggs: Eggs are an excellent source of protein for many dogs, but for those with allergies, they can cause itching, gastrointestinal issues, or even severe reactions.

5. Preservatives and Additives: Artificial additives, preservatives, and food colorings can also be triggers for allergies in dogs. It's wise to steer clear of heavily processed foods containing these ingredients.

6. Common Allergen-Containing Foods: Keep an eye out for ingredients like soybean oil, wheat gluten, and meat by-products on labels, as these can contain common allergens.

ALLERGIC REACTIONS IN DOGS

Recognizing allergic reactions in your dog is crucial for their well-being. Allergic symptoms can vary widely from one dog to another, but here are some common signs to watch for:

1. Itchy Skin: Scratching, licking, or biting themselves excessively can be a sign of skin allergies. Redness, rashes, or hives may also appear.

2. Digestive Issues: Allergic reactions can lead to upset stomachs, diarrhea, vomiting, and excessive gas.

3. Ear Infections: If your dog frequently develops ear infections, it could be due to food allergies.

4. Respiratory Problems: In some cases, dogs may experience coughing, sneezing, or wheezing as a result of allergies.

5. Behavioral Changes: Allergies can make your dog irritable or lethargic. They might become less active or exhibit changes in their behavior.

6. Swelling: Facial swelling, especially around the eyes and muzzle, can indicate an allergic reaction.

IMPORTANCE OF ALLERGEN-FREE DOG FOOD

Now that we've explored the common food allergens and potential allergic reactions in dogs, let's emphasize the significance of providing allergen-free food for your furry companion.

An allergen-free diet can:

1. Relieve Discomfort: Eliminating allergens from your dog's diet can alleviate the discomfort and pain associated with allergies, leading to a happier and healthier pup.

2. Prevent Chronic Issues: Untreated allergies can lead to chronic skin problems, ear infections, and gastrointestinal issues. Providing allergen-free food can prevent these ongoing health concerns.

3. Enhance Quality of Life: A diet tailored to your dog's specific needs can improve their overall quality of life. They'll have more energy, better coat health, and a stronger immune system.

4. Reduce Veterinary Costs: By proactively managing your dog's allergies through their diet, you can potentially reduce the need for frequent visits to the vet and expensive treatments.

As you continue through this cookbook, you'll learn how to create delicious, allergen-free meals that will not only keep your dog safe but also ensure their nutritional needs are met. Armed with this knowledge, you'll be better equipped to address your dog's food allergies and provide them with a happier, healthier life.

CHAPTER 3
Cooking Basics

ESSENTIAL INGREDIENTS AND TOOLS

Before we start crafting delicious allergy-friendly meals for your furry friend, let's go over the essential ingredients and tools you'll need in your dog food cooking arsenal.

Ingredients:

- **Proteins:** Lean meats like chicken, turkey, and lean beef are excellent choices. For variety, you can also use fish, such as salmon or cod. Make sure they are boneless and skinless.
- **Carbohydrates:** Opt for grains like brown rice, quinoa, and oats, or carbohydrate sources like sweet potatoes and pumpkin.
- **Vegetables:** Incorporate vegetables like carrots, green beans, peas, and spinach. These add fiber and essential nutrients.
- **Fruits**: Some fruits, like apples and blueberries, can be included in moderation for added flavor and nutrition.
- **Fats**: Healthy fats like olive oil or coconut oil can be used to provide essential fatty acids.
- **Supplements:** Depending on your dog's specific needs, you may need to add supplements such as calcium or omega-3 fatty acids.

Tools:

- **Cooking Utensils:** Standard kitchen tools such as knives, cutting boards, and mixing bowls will come in handy.
- **Pots and Pans**: You'll need pots and pans for cooking and preparing ingredients.
- **Blender or Food Processor:** These are helpful for pureeing vegetables and creating smoother textures.
- **Food Scale:** A food scale ensures accurate portioning and recipe consistency.
- **Storage Containers:** Invest in airtight storage containers for storing homemade dog food safely.
- **Pet-Friendly Bowls:** Consider using stainless steel or ceramic bowls for serving your dog's meals. These are easy to clean and less likely to harbor bacteria than plastic.

SAFE FOOD HANDLING FOR DOGS

Food safety is just as important for your dog as it is for you. Here are some key practices to keep in mind:

- **Cleanliness:** Wash your hands, utensils, and surfaces thoroughly before and after handling dog food.
- **Safe Ingredient Sourcing**: Choose high-quality, fresh ingredients, and ensure they are safe for your dog to consume.

Avoid ingredients that are toxic to dogs, like onions, garlic, and grapes.

- **Proper Storage**: Store ingredients and prepared dog food in airtight containers in the refrigerator or freezer to prevent spoilage and contamination.
- **Cook Thoroughly:** Cook all meat thoroughly to eliminate the risk of harmful bacteria. Avoid using raw meat in your dog's meals.
- **Avoid Cross-Contamination:** Use separate cutting boards and utensils for dog food preparation to prevent cross-contamination with human food.
- **Balance and Variety:** Ensure your dog's diet is balanced and includes a variety of ingredients to provide all the essential nutrients.

TRANSITIONING TO HOMEMADE FOOD

If your dog has been primarily eating commercial dog food, transitioning to homemade food should be done gradually to prevent digestive upset. Here's a simple guideline:

1. Start by replacing a small portion of your dog's regular food with homemade food, about 10-20% of their total daily intake.

2. Gradually increase the amount of homemade food while decreasing the commercial food over the course of about a week or longer.
3. Monitor your dog for any signs of digestive discomfort during the transition. If they experience diarrhea or other issues, slow down the transition or consult your vet.
4. Once your dog is comfortably eating a diet of homemade food, you can fully transition to your customized allergy-friendly recipes.

CHAPTER 4
Allergy-Friendly Ingredients

PROTEINS: CHOOSING THE RIGHT MEAT

Proteins are the building blocks of a healthy dog diet, but when dealing with food allergies, it's crucial to select meats that are less likely to trigger allergic reactions. Here are some excellent protein options for allergy-friendly meals:

- **Turkey:** Lean and easily digestible, turkey is a great choice for dogs with sensitive stomachs.
- **Lamb:** Often recommended for dogs with common poultry or beef allergies, lamb is a novel protein source that may be less allergenic.
- **Fish:** Salmon and trout are rich in omega-3 fatty acids, which can help soothe skin allergies. Just be cautious of fish bones.
- **Duck:** Duck is another novel protein source that can be gentler on sensitive stomachs.
- **Venison:** Like lamb, venison is less commonly used in dog food and may be a suitable alternative for dogs with allergies to more traditional proteins.

CARBOHYDRATE OPTIONS

Carbohydrates provide energy and fiber in your dog's diet. Here are some allergy-friendly carbohydrate sources to consider:

- **Sweet Potatoes:** Packed with nutrients and fiber, sweet potatoes are easily digestible and a good source of complex carbohydrates.
- **Pumpkin:** High in fiber and low in allergens, pumpkin is excellent for digestive health.
- **Brown Rice:** Brown rice is a gentle grain that's less likely to cause allergies compared to wheat or corn.
- **Quinoa:** Gluten-free and protein-rich, quinoa is an excellent choice for dogs with grain allergies.
- **Oats:** Rolled oats are a source of soluble fiber and can be used to add texture to dog food.

HEALTHY FATS AND OILS

Healthy fats and oils are essential for your dog's skin and coat health, and they can also provide anti-inflammatory benefits. Consider these options:

- **Olive Oil:** Rich in monounsaturated fats, olive oil can help maintain a healthy coat and skin.

- **Coconut Oil:** Coconut oil is not only a source of healthy fats but also contains lauric acid, which can boost the immune system.
- **Fish Oil:** Omega-3 fatty acids found in fish oil can reduce inflammation and alleviate skin allergies.

FRUITS AND VEGETABLES

Fruits and vegetables are excellent sources of vitamins and antioxidants. Here are some dog-friendly options:

- **Carrots:** These crunchy vegetables are low in calories and high in vitamins.
- **Green Beans:** A good source of fiber, green beans can help with digestion.
- **Blueberries:** Rich in antioxidants, blueberries can support overall health.
- **Apples (without seeds):** Apples are a source of fiber and can help clean teeth.

HERBS AND SUPPLEMENTS FOR ALLERGY RELIEF

Certain herbs and supplements can help alleviate allergy symptoms and boost your dog's overall health:

- **Nettle:** Nettle has natural anti-inflammatory properties and can be used as a supplement to soothe allergies.

- **Quercetin:** This antioxidant can help reduce allergic reactions and is often found in supplement form.
- **Probiotics:** Probiotics can support a healthy gut and boost the immune system, which can be beneficial for dogs with food allergies.
- **Omega-3 Fatty Acids:** As mentioned earlier, fish oil supplements are rich in omega-3 fatty acids, which can reduce inflammation and help with skin allergies.

By carefully selecting and incorporating these allergy-friendly ingredients into your homemade dog food recipes, you'll be well on your way to providing your furry friend with meals that are not only delicious but also safe and supportive of their unique dietary needs. In the upcoming chapters, we'll put these ingredients to good use in a variety of recipes designed to cater to different allergies and sensitivities.

CHAPTER 5
Breakfast and Brunch Recipes

HOMEMADE BREAKFAST BOWLS

1. Chicken and Rice Sunrise Bowl

Cook Time: 25 minutes

Servings: 2

Ingredients:

- 1/2 cup cooked chicken breast, shredded
- 1/2 cup cooked brown rice
- 1/4 cup cooked peas
- 1/4 teaspoon olive oil (optional)
- 1 tablespoon fresh cilantro, chopped (for garnish)

Instructions:

1. Combine the cooked chicken breast, cooked brown rice, and cooked peas in a bowl.
2. Drizzle with olive oil (if desired) for added flavor.
3. Garnish with fresh cilantro. Serve when cooled.

Nutritional Information (per serving): Calories: 190, Protein: 15g, Fat: 4g, Carbohydrates: 20g, Fiber: 3g

2. Turkey and Sweet Potato Delight Bowl

Cook Time: 25 minutes

Servings: 2

Ingredients:

- 1/2 cup lean ground turkey
- 1/2 cup mashed sweet potatoes
- 1/4 cup steamed green beans, chopped
- 1/4 teaspoon olive oil (optional)

Instructions:

1. In a skillet over medium heat, cook the ground turkey until fully cooked, breaking it into small pieces. Drain any excess fat.
2. Combine the cooked turkey, mashed sweet potatoes, and steamed green beans in a bowl.
3. Drizzle with olive oil (if desired) for added healthy fats.
4. Serve when cooled.

Nutritional Information (per serving): Calories: 190, Protein: 12g, Fat: 8g, Carbohydrates: 17g, Fiber: 4g

3. Salmon and Quinoa Sunrise Bowl

Cook Time: 20 minutes

Servings: 2

Ingredients:

- 1/2 cup cooked salmon, flaked (bones and skin removed)
- 1/2 cup cooked quinoa
- 1/4 cup steamed carrots, diced
- 1/4 teaspoon coconut oil (optional)
- 1 teaspoon fresh dill, chopped (for garnish)

Instructions:

1. Combine the cooked salmon, cooked quinoa, and steamed carrots in a bowl.
2. Drizzle with coconut oil (if desired) for added flavor and healthy fats.
3. Garnish with fresh dill.
4. Serve when cooled.

Nutritional Information (per serving): Calories: 220, Protein: 16g, Fat: 6g, Carbohydrates: 23g, Fiber: 3g

4. Venison and Pumpkin Delight Bowl

Cook Time: 30 minutes

Servings: 2

Ingredients:

- 1/2 cup cooked venison, diced
- 1/2 cup canned pumpkin (unsweetened)
- 1/4 cup cooked green beans, chopped
- 1/4 teaspoon flaxseed oil (optional)
- 1 teaspoon fresh thyme leaves (for garnish)

Instructions:

1. Combine the cooked venison, canned pumpkin, and cooked green beans in a bowl.
2. Drizzle with flaxseed oil (if desired) for added omega-3 fatty acids.
3. Garnish with fresh thyme leaves.
4. Serve when cooled.

Nutritional Information (per serving): Calories: 170, Protein: 14g, Fat: 5g, Carbohydrates: 16g, Fiber: 5g

OMELETS AND SCRAMBLES

5. Salmon and Spinach Scramble

Cook Time: 15 minutes

Servings: 2

Ingredients:

- 1/2 cup canned salmon (boneless and skinless)
- 1/4 cup fresh spinach, finely chopped
- 2 eggs
- 1/4 teaspoon olive oil (for cooking)
- Fresh parsley (for garnish)

Instructions:

1. In a bowl, whisk the eggs until well beaten.
2. Heat olive oil in a skillet over medium heat.
3. Add the chopped spinach and sauté for 2 minutes until wilted.
4. Pour in the whisked eggs and canned salmon.
5. Gently scramble the mixture until the eggs are fully cooked.
6. Garnish with fresh parsley.
7. Cool before serving.

Nutritional Information (per serving): Calories: 160, Protein: 15g, Fat: 7g, Carbohydrates: 1g, Fiber: 0.5g

6. Turkey and Sweet Potato Omelet

Cook Time: 20 minutes

Servings: 2

Ingredients:

- 1/2 cup lean ground turkey
- 1/2 cup cooked sweet potatoes, diced
- 2 eggs
- 1/4 teaspoon coconut oil (for cooking)
- Fresh thyme leaves (for garnish)

Instructions:

1. In a skillet over medium heat, cook the ground turkey until fully cooked.
2. Add the diced sweet potatoes and continue cooking until they're tender and slightly caramelized.
3. In a separate pan, heat the coconut oil over medium heat.
4. Pour in the whisked eggs to make an omelet.
5. Once the omelet is set, add the cooked turkey and sweet potatoes on one half and fold the other half over.
6. Garnish with fresh thyme leaves. Cool before serving.

Nutritional Information (per serving): Calories: 190, Protein: 16g, Fat: 9g, Carbohydrates: 10g, Fiber: 2g

7. Veggie Delight Scramble

Cook Time: 15 minutes

Servings: 2

Ingredients:

- 1/2 cup cooked lean ground beef
- 1/4 cup broccoli florets, finely chopped
- 1/4 cup red bell pepper, diced
- 2 eggs
- 1/4 teaspoon olive oil (for cooking)

Instructions:

1. In a skillet over medium heat, cook the lean ground beef until fully cooked.
2. Add the chopped broccoli and red bell pepper and sauté until tender.
3. In a separate pan, heat the olive oil over medium heat.
4. Pour in the whisked eggs and scramble until fully cooked.
5. Combine the cooked beef and vegetables with the scrambled eggs. Cool before serving.

Nutritional Information (per serving): Calories: 180, Protein: 15g, Fat: 9g, Carbohydrates: 5g, Fiber: 2g

8. Chicken and Zucchini Omelet

Cook Time: 20 minutes

Servings: 2

Ingredients:

- 1/2 cup cooked chicken breast, diced
- 1/4 cup zucchini, grated
- 2 eggs
- 1/4 teaspoon coconut oil (for cooking)
- Fresh parsley (for garnish)

Instructions:

1. In a skillet over medium heat, sauté the grated zucchini until it's slightly softened.
2. Add the diced chicken breast and continue cooking until heated through.
3. In a separate pan, heat the coconut oil over medium heat.
4. Pour in the whisked eggs to make an omelet.
5. Once the omelet is set, add the cooked chicken and zucchini on one half and fold the other half over.
6. Garnish with fresh parsley. Cool before serving.

Nutritional Information (per serving): Calories: 160, Protein: 15g, Fat: 7g, Carbohydrates: 2g, Fiber: 1g

NUTRITIOUS PANCAKES AND WAFFLES

9. Pumpkin and Cinnamon Pancakes

Cook Time: 15 minutes

Servings: 2

Ingredients:

- 1/2 cup canned pumpkin (unsweetened)
- 1/4 cup oat flour (gluten-free)
- 1/4 teaspoon cinnamon
- 2 eggs
- 1/4 teaspoon coconut oil (for cooking)

Instructions:

1. In a bowl, combine the canned pumpkin, oat flour, cinnamon, and eggs to make the pancake batter.
2. Heat a non-stick skillet over medium heat and add the coconut oil.
3. Pour small portions of the batter onto the skillet to form pancakes.
4. Cook until bubbles form on the surface, then flip and cook the other side until golden brown.
5. Cool slightly before serving.

Nutritional Information (per serving): Calories: 150, Protein: 7g, Fat: 7g, Carbohydrates: 15g, Fiber: 3g

10. Banana and Peanut Butter Waffles

Cook Time: 15 minutes

Servings: 2

Ingredients:

- 1 ripe banana, mashed
- 2 tablespoons natural peanut butter (unsalted)
- 1 egg
- 1/4 cup coconut flour
- 1/4 teaspoon baking powder

Instructions:

1. In a bowl, combine the mashed banana, peanut butter, egg, coconut flour, and baking powder to make the waffle batter.
2. Preheat your waffle iron according to the manufacturer's instructions.
3. Lightly grease the waffle iron with a small amount of coconut oil.
4. Pour the batter onto the waffle iron and cook until golden brown and crisp.
5. Let the waffles cool slightly before serving.

Nutritional Information (per serving): Calories: 180, Protein: 6g, Fat: 8g, Carbohydrates: 22g, Fiber: 6g

11. Spinach and Cheese Pancakes

Cook Time: 20 minutes

Servings: 2

Ingredients:

- 1/2 cup fresh spinach, finely chopped
- 1/4 cup low-fat cottage cheese
- 2 eggs
- 2 tablespoons oat flour (gluten-free)
- 1/4 teaspoon olive oil (for cooking)

Instructions:

1. In a bowl, combine the chopped spinach, cottage cheese, eggs, and oat flour to make the pancake batter.
2. Heat a non-stick skillet over medium heat and add the olive oil.
3. Pour small portions of the batter onto the skillet to form pancakes.
4. Cook until the edges are set and the bottoms are golden brown, then flip and cook the other side until cooked through.
5. Cool slightly before serving.

Nutritional Information (per serving): Calories: 150, Protein: 10g, Fat: 7g, Carbohydrates: 9g, Fiber: 1g

12. Blueberry Oat Waffles

Cook Time: 20 minutes

Servings: 2

Ingredients:

- 1/2 cup rolled oats (gluten-free)
- 2 tablespoons fresh blueberries, mashed
- 1 egg
- 1/4 teaspoon baking powder

Instructions:

1. In a blender or food processor, grind the rolled oats into a fine flour.
2. In a bowl, combine the oat flour, mashed blueberries, egg, and baking powder to make the waffle batter.
3. Preheat your waffle iron according to the manufacturer's instructions.
4. Lightly grease the waffle iron with a small amount of coconut oil.
5. Pour the batter onto the waffle iron and cook until golden brown and crisp. Cool before serving.

Nutritional Information (per serving): Calories: 170, Protein: 7g, Fat: 5g, Carbohydrates: 23g, Fiber: 4g

CHAPTER 6
Lunch and Dinner Delights

PROTEIN-PACKED ENTREES

13. Salmon and Potato Delight

Cook Time: 30 minutes

Servings: 4

Ingredients:

- 1 cup cooked salmon, flaked (bones and skin removed)
- 1/2 cup cooked potatoes, diced
- 1/4 cup carrots, cooked and diced
- 1/4 cup zucchini, cooked and diced
- 1/4 teaspoon fish oil (optional)

Instructions:

1. Combine the cooked salmon, cooked diced potatoes, cooked diced carrots, and cooked diced zucchini in a bowl.
2. Drizzle with fish oil (if desired) for added omega-3s.
3. Mix well and cool before serving.

Nutritional Information (per serving): Calories: 170, Protein: 14g, Fat: 5g, Carbohydrates: 16g, Fiber: 4g

14. Chicken and Rice Stew

Cook Time: 40 minutes

Servings: 4

Ingredients:

- 1 cup cooked chicken breast, diced
- 1/2 cup cooked brown rice
- 1/4 cup peas, cooked and mashed
- 1/4 cup carrots, cooked and diced
- 1/4 cup low-sodium chicken broth

Instructions:

1. In a pot, combine the cooked chicken, cooked brown rice, mashed peas, diced carrots, and chicken broth.
2. Cook over low heat for 20-30 minutes, allowing the flavors to meld and the stew to thicken.
3. Cool to an appropriate temperature before serving.

Nutritional Information (per serving): Calories: 190, Protein: 20g, Fat: 2g, Carbohydrates: 20g, Fiber: 3g

15. Turkey and Quinoa Bowl

Cook Time: 30 minutes

Servings: 4

Ingredients:

- 1 cup lean ground turkey
- 1/2 cup cooked quinoa
- 1/4 cup green beans, steamed and chopped
- 1/4 cup sweet potatoes, cooked and mashed
- 1/4 teaspoon olive oil (optional)

Instructions:

1. In a skillet over medium heat, cook the lean ground turkey until fully cooked.
2. Combine the cooked turkey, cooked quinoa, steamed green beans, and mashed sweet potatoes in a bowl.
3. Drizzle with olive oil (if desired) for added flavor and healthy fats.
4. Mix well and let it cool before serving.

Nutritional Information (per serving): Calories: 180, Protein: 15g, Fat: 5g, Carbohydrates: 19g, Fiber: 3g

16. Venison and Pumpkin Stew

Cook Time: 40 minutes

Servings: 4

Ingredients:

- 1 cup cooked venison, diced
- 1/2 cup canned pumpkin (unsweetened)
- 1/4 cup green beans, steamed and chopped
- 1/4 cup carrots, cooked and diced
- 1/4 teaspoon flaxseed oil (optional)

Instructions:

1. In a pot, combine the cooked diced venison, canned pumpkin, steamed green beans, and cooked diced carrots.
2. Drizzle with flaxseed oil (if desired) for added omega-3s.
3. Cook over low heat for 20-30 minutes, allowing the flavors to meld.
4. Cool to an appropriate temperature before serving.

Nutritional Information (per serving): Calories: 160, Protein: 16g, Fat: 5g, Carbohydrates: 14g, Fiber: 3g

GRAIN-FREE SIDE DISHES

17. Cauliflower and Turkey "Rice"

Cook Time: 20 minutes

Servings: 4

Ingredients:

- 1 head cauliflower, florets
- 1/2 cup lean ground turkey
- 1/4 cup carrots, finely diced
- 1/4 cup peas
- 1/4 teaspoon coconut oil (for cooking)

Instructions:

1. In a food processor, pulse the cauliflower florets until they resemble rice.
2. In a skillet over medium heat, sauté the lean ground turkey in coconut oil until fully cooked.
3. Add the finely diced carrots and peas, and cook until tender.
4. Stir in the cauliflower "rice" and cook for an additional 5 minutes. Cool before serving.

Nutritional Information (per serving): Calories: 80, Protein: 7g, Fat: 2g, Carbohydrates: 9g, Fiber: 4g

18. Zucchini Noodles with Chicken

Cook Time: 15 minutes

Servings: 4

Ingredients:

- 4 medium zucchinis, spiralized into noodles
- 1 cup cooked chicken breast, shredded
- 1/4 cup cherry tomatoes, halved
- 1/4 cup fresh basil leaves, chopped
- 1/4 teaspoon olive oil (for cooking)

Instructions:

1. In a skillet over medium heat, add the olive oil and spiralized zucchini noodles.
2. Sauté for 5-7 minutes until tender.
3. Stir in the shredded chicken, halved cherry tomatoes, and chopped fresh basil.
4. Cook for an additional 2-3 minutes until heated through.
5. Cool before serving.

Nutritional Information (per serving): Calories: 90, Protein: 15g, Fat: 2g, Carbohydrates: 8g, Fiber: 3g

19. Broccoli and Salmon Medley

Cook Time: 20 minutes

Servings: 4

Ingredients:

- 1 cup cooked salmon, flaked (bones and skin removed)
- 2 cups broccoli florets, steamed and chopped
- 1/4 cup carrots, steamed and diced
- 1/4 cup zucchini, steamed and diced
- 1/4 teaspoon fish oil (optional)

Instructions:

1. Combine the cooked salmon, steamed and chopped broccoli florets, steamed diced carrots, and steamed diced zucchini in a bowl.
2. Drizzle with fish oil (if desired) for added omega-3s.
3. Mix well and cool before serving.

Nutritional Information (per serving): Calories: 130, Protein: 15g, Fat: 5g, Carbohydrates: 8g, Fiber: 3g

20. Pumpkin and Green Bean Delight

Cook Time: 15 minutes

Servings: 4

Ingredients:

- 1/2 cup canned pumpkin (unsweetened)
- 1 cup green beans, steamed and chopped
- 1/4 cup carrots, steamed and diced
- 1/4 teaspoon flaxseed oil (optional)

Instructions:

1. In a bowl, combine the canned pumpkin, steamed and chopped green beans, and steamed diced carrots.
2. Drizzle with flaxseed oil (if desired) for added omega-3s.
3. Mix well and cool before serving.

Nutritional Information (per serving): Calories: 45, Protein: 1g, Fat: 1g, Carbohydrates: 10g, Fiber: 3g

VEGETABLE-CENTRIC MEALS

21. Quinoa and Veggie Stir-Fry

Cook Time: 25 minutes

Servings: 4

Ingredients:

- 1 cup cooked quinoa
- 1 cup broccoli florets, steamed
- 1/2 cup red bell pepper, thinly sliced
- 1/2 cup snap peas, chopped
- 1/4 cup carrots, julienned
- 1/4 cup low-sodium vegetable broth

Instructions:

1. In a skillet over medium heat, combine the cooked quinoa, steamed broccoli florets, thinly sliced red bell pepper, chopped snap peas, and julienned carrots.
2. Pour in the low-sodium vegetable broth and cook for 5-7 minutes until the vegetables are tender.
3. Cool before serving.

Nutritional Information (per serving): Calories: 130, Protein: 5g, Fat: 1g, Carbohydrates: 28g, Fiber: 5g

22. Spinach and Chickpea Delight

Cook Time: 20 minutes

Servings: 4

Ingredients:

- 2 cups fresh spinach leaves
- 1 cup canned chickpeas (unsalted), rinsed and drained
- 1/2 cup zucchini, diced
- 1/2 cup carrots, diced
- 1/4 cup low-sodium vegetable broth
- 1/4 teaspoon olive oil (optional)

Instructions:

1. In a skillet over medium heat, add the olive oil and fresh spinach leaves.
2. Sauté for 2-3 minutes until wilted.
3. Add the diced zucchini, diced carrots, canned chickpeas, and low-sodium vegetable broth.
4. Cook for an additional 5-7 minutes until the vegetables are tender.
5. Cool before serving.

Nutritional Information (per serving): Calories: 130, Protein: 6g, Fat: 1g, Carbohydrates: 24g, Fiber: 6g

23. Sweet Potato and Green Bean Bowl

Cook Time: 25 minutes

Servings: 4

Ingredients:

- 2 cups sweet potatoes, peeled and diced
- 1 cup green beans, steamed and chopped
- 1/2 cup peas, steamed
- 1/4 cup low-sodium vegetable broth
- 1/4 teaspoon coconut oil (optional)

Instructions:

1. In a pot, add the diced sweet potatoes and cover with water.
2. Boil until the sweet potatoes are tender, then drain.
3. In a skillet over medium heat, combine the cooked sweet potatoes, steamed and chopped green beans, steamed peas, and low-sodium vegetable broth.
4. Cook for 5-7 minutes until heated through.
5. Drizzle with coconut oil (if desired) for added flavor.
6. Cool before serving.

Nutritional Information (per serving): Calories: 120, Protein: 3g, Fat: 1g, Carbohydrates: 28g, Fiber: 5g

24. Butternut Squash and Kale Medley

Cook Time: 30 minutes

Servings: 4

Ingredients:

- 2 cups butternut squash, peeled and diced
- 2 cups kale leaves, chopped
- 1/2 cup white beans, cooked and drained
- 1/4 cup low-sodium vegetable broth
- 1/4 teaspoon olive oil (optional)

Instructions:

1. In a skillet over medium heat, add the olive oil and diced butternut squash.
2. Sauté for 5-7 minutes until the squash is tender.
3. Stir in the chopped kale leaves, cooked and drained white beans, and low-sodium vegetable broth.
4. Cook for an additional 5 minutes until the kale is wilted.
5. Cool before serving.

Nutritional Information (per serving): Calories: 110, Protein: 4g, Fat: 1g, Carbohydrates: 24g, Fiber: 6g

CHAPTER 7
Tasty Treats and Snacks

ALLERGY-FRIENDLY BISCUITS

25. Blueberry and Oat Biscuits

Cook Time: 25 minutes

Servings: Approx. 24 small biscuits

Ingredients:

- 1/2 cup fresh blueberries, mashed
- 1/2 cup rolled oats (gluten-free)
- 1 1/2 cups brown rice flour
- 1/4 cup water

Instructions:

1. Preheat your oven to 350°F (175°C) and line a baking sheet with parchment paper.
2. In a bowl, combine the mashed fresh blueberries, rolled oats, brown rice flour, and water.
3. Mix until you have a dough.
4. Roll out the dough to about 1/4-inch thickness and cut into small biscuit shapes.

5. Place the biscuits on the prepared baking sheet and bake for 15-20 minutes until they are slightly crispy.
6. Cool completely before serving.

Nutritional Information (per serving - 1 biscuit): Calories: 25, Protein: 1g, Fat: 0.5g, Carbohydrates: 5g, Fiber: 1g

26. Carrot and Cheddar Crunchies

Cook Time: 30 minutes

Servings: Approx. 24 small crunchies

Ingredients:

- 1 cup carrots, grated
- 1/2 cup cheddar cheese, shredded
- 1 1/2 cups brown rice flour
- 1/4 cup water

Instructions:

1. Preheat your oven to 350°F (175°C) and line a baking sheet with parchment paper.
2. In a bowl, combine the grated carrots, shredded cheddar cheese, brown rice flour, and water.
3. Mix until you have a dough.
4. Roll out the dough to about 1/4-inch thickness and cut into small crunchie shapes.
5. Place the crunchies on the prepared baking sheet and bake for 20-25 minutes until crispy.
6. Cool completely before serving.

Nutritional Information (per serving - 1 crunchie): Calories: 30, Protein: 1g, Fat: 1g, Carbohydrates: 4g, Fiber: 0.5g

27. Apple and Cinnamon Biscuits

Cook Time: 20 minutes

Servings: Approx. 24 small biscuits

Ingredients:

- 1 cup apples, peeled, cored, and finely chopped
- 1 1/2 cups coconut flour
- 1/4 teaspoon cinnamon
- 1/4 cup water

Instructions:

1. Preheat your oven to 350°F (175°C) and line a baking sheet with parchment paper.
2. In a bowl, combine the finely chopped apples, coconut flour, and cinnamon.
3. Gradually add water, mixing until you have a dough.
4. Roll out the dough to about 1/4-inch thickness and cut into small biscuit shapes.
5. Place the biscuits on the prepared baking sheet and bake for 15-18 minutes until they turn golden.
6. Cool completely before serving.

Nutritional Information (per serving - 1 biscuit): Calories: 25, Protein: 1g, Fat: 0.5g, Carbohydrates: 5g, Fiber: 2g

28. Salmon and Sweet Potato Bites

Cook Time: 30 minutes

Servings: Approx. 24 small bites

Ingredients:

- 1/2 cup canned salmon (boneless and skinless), drained
- 1/2 cup sweet potato, cooked and mashed
- 1 1/2 cups garbanzo bean flour (chickpea flour)
- 1/4 cup water

Instructions:

1. Preheat your oven to 350°F (175°C) and line a baking sheet with parchment paper.
2. In a bowl, combine the canned salmon, mashed sweet potato, garbanzo bean flour, and water.
3. Mix until you have a dough.
4. Roll the dough into small bite-sized pieces and place them on the prepared baking sheet.
5. Bake for 20-25 minutes until they are firm and slightly crispy.
6. Cool completely before serving.

Nutritional Information (per serving - 1 bite): Calories: 20, Protein: 1g, Fat: 0.5g, Carbohydrates: 3g, Fiber: 0.5g

CHEWY AND CRUNCHY SNACKS

29. Chewy Sweet Potato Slices

Cook Time: 2 hours (including drying time)

Servings: Varies based on sweet potato size

Ingredients:

- 2 large sweet potatoes

Instructions:

1. Preheat your oven to 250°F (120°C).
2. Wash and peel the sweet potatoes.
3. Slice them into thin rounds, about 1/4 inch thick.
4. Place the slices on a baking sheet lined with parchment paper.
5. Bake for 2 hours or until the slices become chewy. Turn them over halfway through.
6. Allow them to cool completely before serving.

Nutritional Information (per serving - 1 slice): Calories: 10, Protein: 0.2g, Fat: 0g, Carbohydrates: 2.4g, Fiber: 0.4g

30. Crunchy Apple Chips

Cook Time: 3 hours (including drying time)

Servings: Varies based on apple size

Ingredients:

- 2-3 apples (any variety)

Instructions:

1. Preheat your oven to 200°F (95°C).
2. Wash and core the apples, leaving the skin intact for added fiber.
3. Slice the apples into thin rounds, about 1/8 inch thick.
4. Place the slices on a baking sheet lined with parchment paper.
5. Bake for 3 hours or until the chips are crispy. Rotate the trays and flip the slices halfway through.
6. Let them cool completely before offering them as a snack.

Nutritional Information (per serving - 1 chip): Calories: 5, Protein: 0g, Fat: 0g, Carbohydrates: 1.5g, Fiber: 0.2g

31. Chewy Chicken Jerky

Cook Time: 3 hours

Servings: Varies based on chicken breast size

Ingredients:

- 2 boneless, skinless chicken breasts

Instructions:

1. Preheat your oven to 200°F (95°C).
2. Slice the chicken breasts into long, thin strips, about 1/4 inch wide.
3. Place the chicken strips on a baking sheet lined with parchment paper.
4. Bake for 3 hours or until the strips become chewy but not brittle.
5. Allow them to cool completely before serving.

Nutritional Information (per serving - 1 strip): Calories: 10, Protein: 1g, Fat: 0g, Carbohydrates: 0g, Fiber: 0g

32. Crunchy Carrot Sticks

Cook Time: 2 hours (including drying time)

Servings: Varies based on carrot size

Ingredients:

- 4-6 fresh carrots

Instructions:

1. Preheat your oven to 250°F (120°C).
2. Wash and peel the carrots.
3. Cut the carrots into sticks or rounds, whichever your dog prefers.
4. Place the carrot pieces on a baking sheet lined with parchment paper.
5. Bake for 2 hours or until the carrots become crunchy. Turn them over halfway through.
6. Cool thoroughly before offering them as a crunchy snack.

Nutritional Information (per serving - 1 stick): Calories: 5, Protein: 0.1g, Fat: 0g, Carbohydrates: 1.3g, Fiber: 0.4g

FROZEN TREATS FOR HOT DAYS

33. Banana and Blueberry Pupsicles

Prep Time: 10 minutes

Freeze Time: 3 hours

Servings: 6 popsicles

Ingredients:

- 1 ripe banana
- 1/2 cup fresh blueberries
- 1 cup plain Greek yogurt (unsweetened, unflavored)

Instructions:

1. In a blender, combine the ripe banana, fresh blueberries, and plain Greek yogurt.
2. Blend until smooth.
3. Pour the mixture into popsicle molds or ice cube trays.
4. Freeze for at least 3 hours until solid.
5. Remove from molds or trays and let your pup enjoy!

Nutritional Information (per serving - 1 popsicle): Calories: 30, Protein: 2g, Fat: 0.5g, Carbohydrates: 6g, Fiber: 1g

34. Peanut Butter and Banana Frosty Paws

Prep Time: 10 minutes

Freeze Time: 4 hours

Servings: 4 servings

Ingredients:

- 2 ripe bananas
- 1/2 cup natural peanut butter (unsalted)
- 1 cup plain yogurt (unsweetened, unflavored)

Instructions:

1. In a blender, combine the ripe bananas, natural peanut butter, and plain yogurt.
2. Blend until the mixture is smooth.
3. Pour the mixture into ice cube trays or silicone molds.
4. Freeze for at least 4 hours until solid.
5. Serve to your pup for a tasty, cool treat.

Nutritional Information (per serving): Calories: 180, Protein: 6g, Fat: 12g, Carbohydrates: 13g, Fiber: 2g

35. Watermelon and Mint Coolers

Prep Time: 10 minutes

Freeze Time: 3 hours

Servings: 8 servings

Ingredients:

- 2 cups seedless watermelon, cubed
- 1 tablespoon fresh mint leaves, chopped
- 1 cup coconut water (unsweetened)

Instructions:

1. In a blender, combine the seedless watermelon, fresh mint leaves, and coconut water.
2. Blend until smooth.
3. Pour the mixture into ice cube trays or silicone molds.
4. Freeze for at least 3 hours until solid.
5. Let your dog savor the refreshing taste!

Nutritional Information (per serving - 2 cubes): Calories: 15, Protein: 0.5g, Fat: 0g, Carbohydrates: 4g, Fiber: 0.5g

36. Chicken and Vegetable Ice Lollies

Prep Time: 15 minutes

Freeze Time: 4 hours

Servings: 6 lollies

Ingredients:

- 1 cup cooked chicken breast, shredded
- 1/2 cup mixed vegetables (carrots, peas, green beans), cooked and chopped
- 1 cup low-sodium chicken broth

Instructions:

1. In a bowl, combine the cooked chicken breast, mixed vegetables, and low-sodium chicken broth.
2. Mix well.
3. Pour the mixture into ice lolly molds or small paper cups.
4. Freeze for at least 4 hours until they are frozen solid.
5. Remove from the molds or cups and let your dog enjoy this savory frozen delight!

Nutritional Information (per serving - 1 lolly): Calories: 45, Protein: 6g, Fat: 1g, Carbohydrates: 2g, Fiber: 0.5g

37. Yogurt and Berry Bark

Prep Time: 10 minutes

Freeze Time: 3 hours

Servings: 8 servings

Ingredients:

- 1 cup plain Greek yogurt (unsweetened, unflavored)
- 1/2 cup mixed berries (blueberries, strawberries, raspberries), chopped

Instructions:

1. In a bowl, combine the plain Greek yogurt and chopped mixed berries.
2. Mix until well combined.
3. Spread the mixture evenly on a baking sheet lined with parchment paper.
4. Freeze for at least 3 hours until it's firm.
5. Break the bark into smaller pieces and let your dog savor this tasty, frosty treat!

Nutritional Information (per serving - 1 piece): Calories: 20, Protein: 2g, Fat: 0.5g, Carbohydrates: 2.5g, Fiber: 0.5g

CHAPTER 8

Special Occasion and Celebration Meals

BIRTHDAY CAKES AND PUPCAKES

38. Peanut Butter and Banana Pupcake

Prep Time: 15 minutes

Bake Time: 20 minutes

Servings: 4 pupcakes

Ingredients:

- 1 ripe banana, mashed
- 1/4 cup natural peanut butter (unsalted)
- 1/4 cup unsweetened applesauce
- 1 cup brown rice flour
- 1 teaspoon baking powder
- 1/4 cup water

Instructions:

1. Preheat your oven to 350°F (175°C) and line a muffin tin with cupcake liners.

2. In a bowl, combine the mashed banana, natural peanut butter, and unsweetened applesauce.
3. Add brown rice flour and baking powder to the mixture and stir well.
4. Gradually add water, mixing until you have a smooth batter.
5. Pour the batter evenly into the cupcake liners.
6. Bake for 20 minutes or until a toothpick comes out clean.
7. Let the pupcakes cool completely before serving.

Nutritional Information (per pupcake): Calories: 160, Protein: 4g, Fat: 6g, Carbohydrates: 23g, Fiber: 2g

39. Carrot and Cream Cheese Birthday Cake

Prep Time: 20 minutes **Bake Time:** 25 minutes

Servings: 6 slices

Ingredients:

- 1 cup carrots, grated
- 1/4 cup unsweetened applesauce
- 1/4 cup natural cream cheese (unsalted)
- 1 cup brown rice flour
- 1 teaspoon baking powder
- 1/4 cup water

Instructions:

1. Preheat your oven to 350°F (175°C) and grease a small cake pan.
2. In a bowl, combine the grated carrots, unsweetened applesauce, and natural cream cheese.
3. Add brown rice flour and baking powder to the mixture and stir well. Gradually add water, mixing until you have a smooth cake batter. Pour the batter into the greased cake pan.
4. Bake for 25 minutes or until a toothpick comes out clean.
5. Let the cake cool before slicing it into six pieces.

Nutritional Information (per slice): Calories: 120, Protein: 3g, Fat: 3g, Carbohydrates: 20g, Fiber: 2

40. Salmon and Sweet Potato Celebration Cake

Prep Time: 20 minutes **Bake Time:** 30 minutes

Servings: 8 slices

Ingredients:

- 1/2 cup canned salmon (boneless and skinless), drained
- 1/2 cup sweet potato, cooked and mashed
- 1/4 cup natural peanut butter (unsalted)
- 1 cup oat flour (gluten-free)
- 1 teaspoon baking powder
- 1/4 cup water

Instructions:

1. Preheat your oven to 350°F (175°C) and grease a small cake pan.
2. In a bowl, combine the canned salmon, mashed sweet potato, and natural peanut butter.
3. Add oat flour and baking powder to the mixture and stir well.
4. Gradually add water, mixing until you have a smooth cake batter. Pour the batter into the greased cake pan.
5. Bake for 30 minutes or until a toothpick comes out clean.
6. Allow the cake to cool before cutting it into eight slices.

Nutritional Information (per slice): Calories: 90, Protein: 4g, Fat: 3g, Carbohydrates: 11g, Fiber: 2g

41. Blueberry and Coconut Frosting Pupcake

Prep Time: 20 minutes **Bake Time:** 20 minutes

Servings: 4 pupcakes

Ingredients:

- 1/4 cup fresh blueberries, mashed
- 1/4 cup unsweetened applesauce
- 1 cup brown rice flour
- 1 teaspoon baking powder
- 1/4 cup water

Coconut Frosting:

- 1/4 cup plain Greek yogurt (unsweetened, unflavored)
- 2 tablespoons unsweetened shredded coconut

Instructions:

1. Preheat your oven to 350°F (175°C) and line a muffin tin with cupcake liners.
2. In a bowl, combine the mashed fresh blueberries and unsweetened applesauce.
3. Add brown rice flour and baking powder to the mixture and stir well.
4. Gradually add water, mixing until you have a smooth batter.
5. Pour the batter evenly into the cupcake liners.

6. Bake for 20 minutes or until a toothpick comes out clean.
7. While the pupcakes cool, prepare the frosting by mixing plain Greek yogurt and shredded coconut.
8. Once the pupcakes are cooled, frost them with the coconut frosting.

Nutritional Information (per pupcake): Calories: 100, Protein: 2g, Fat: 1.5g, Carbohydrates: 20g, Fiber: 2g

HOLIDAY FEASTS FOR DOGS

42. Thanksgiving Turkey and Sweet Potato Delight

Prep Time: 20 minutes **Cook Time:** 45 minutes

Servings: 4 servings

Ingredients:

- 1 cup cooked turkey meat, diced
- 1/2 cup sweet potato, cooked and mashed
- 1/2 cup green beans, cooked and chopped
- 1/4 cup cranberries, fresh or frozen (unsweetened)

Instructions:

1. Preheat your oven to 350°F (175°C).
2. In a large bowl, combine the diced turkey meat, mashed sweet potato, chopped green beans, and cranberries.
3. Mix well.
4. Scoop the mixture into a greased baking dish.
5. Bake for 45 minutes or until the top is golden and the cranberries have softened. Allow it to cool before serving to your pup.

Nutritional Information (per serving): Calories: 160, Protein: 18g, Fat: 5g, Carbohydrates: 11g, Fiber: 3g

43. Christmas Beef and Potato Casserole.

Prep Time: 20 minutes **Cook Time:** 50 minutes

Servings: 4 servings

Ingredients:

- 1 cup lean ground beef
- 1/2 cup sweet potato, cooked and diced
- 1/2 cup green peas, cooked
- 1/4 cup carrots, cooked and chopped
- 1/4 cup low-sodium beef broth

Instructions:

1. Preheat your oven to 350°F (175°C).
2. In a skillet, cook the lean ground beef until browned. Drain any excess fat.
3. In a large bowl, combine the cooked ground beef, diced sweet potato, cooked green peas, chopped carrots, and low-sodium beef broth. Mix well.
4. Transfer the mixture to a greased casserole dish.
5. Bake for 50 minutes or until it's bubbling and the top is golden.
6. Allow it to cool slightly before serving to your pup.

Nutritional Information (per serving): Calories: 180, Protein: 14g, Fat: 7g, Carbohydrates: 14g, Fiber: 3g

44. Easter Lamb and Spinach Stew

Prep Time: 20 minutes **Cook Time:** 40 minutes

Servings: 4 servings

Ingredients:

- 1 cup lean ground lamb
- 1/2 cup spinach, chopped
- 1/2 cup zucchini, diced
- 1/4 cup carrots, cooked and chopped
- 1/4 cup low-sodium lamb broth

Instructions:

1. In a skillet, cook the lean ground lamb until browned. Drain any excess fat.
2. In a large pot, combine the cooked lamb, chopped spinach, diced zucchini, chopped carrots, and low-sodium lamb broth.
3. Cook over medium heat for 40 minutes, stirring occasionally, until the vegetables are tender.
4. Allow it to cool slightly before serving to your pup.

Nutritional Information (per serving): Calories: 160, Protein: 14g, Fat: 8g, Carbohydrates: 10g, Fiber: 2g

45. Fourth of July Chicken and Pea Pie

Prep Time: 20 minutes **Bake Time:** 35 minutes

Servings: 4 servings

Ingredients:

- 1 cup cooked chicken breast, diced
- 1/2 cup green peas, cooked
- 1/2 cup potatoes, cooked and diced
- 1/4 cup low-sodium chicken broth

Instructions:

1. Preheat your oven to 350°F (175°C).
2. In a large bowl, combine the diced chicken breast, cooked green peas, diced potatoes, and low-sodium chicken broth.
3. Mix well.
4. Transfer the mixture to a greased pie dish.
5. Bake for 35 minutes or until the top is golden and the pie is heated through.
6. Allow it to cool slightly before serving to your pup.

Nutritional Information (per serving): Calories: 140, Protein: 16g, Fat: 3g, Carbohydrates: 10g, Fiber: 2g

14-DAY MEAL PLAN

WEEK 1

DAY	BREAKFAST	LUNCH	DINNER
Day 1	Scrambled Eggs	Turkey and Rice	Baked Chicken with Sweet Potato
Day 2	Oatmeal with Blueberries	Spinach and Salmon	Beef and Vegetable Stew
Day 3	Yogurt with Banana Slices	Tuna Salad	Quinoa and Turkey Meatballs
Day 4	Peanut Butter and Apple Slices	Chicken and Sweet Potato	Fish with Brown Rice
Day 5	Cottage Cheese with Carrots	Turkey and Green Beans	Lamb and Potato Casserole

Day 6	Pumpkin and Rice Porridge	Beef and Broccoli	Pork and Mixed Veggies
Day 7	Chicken and Rice Congee	Salmon and Asparagus	Venison with Pumpkin

WEEK 2

DAY	BREAKFAST	LUNCH	DINNER
Day 8	Scrambled Eggs with Spinach	Tuna and Brown Rice	Chicken and Quinoa
Day 9	Cottage Cheese and Blueberries	Turkey and Carrot Sticks	Beef and Potato Stew
Day 10	Oatmeal with Banana Slices	Salmon and Green Peas	Turkey and Rice Casserole
Day 11	Greek Yogurt with Strawberries	Chicken and Zucchini	Fish with Sweet Potato
Day 12	Peanut Butter and Celery	Lamb and Sweet Potato	Pork and Mixed Greens
Day 13	Pumpkin and Rice Porridge	Beef and Mixed Veggies	Venison with Spinach

| Day 14 | Chicken and Rice Congee | Turkey and Pumpkin | Bison and Mixed Veggies |

CONCLUSION

As we reach the end of this culinary journey through the Dog Food Cookbook for Food Allergies, we hope you've discovered a world of nourishment and healing for your beloved four-legged companion. Your dog's health and happiness are our greatest priorities, and we're thrilled to have shared this path with you.

Remember, this cookbook is not just a collection of recipes; it's a testament to the power of love, care, and the profound impact that tailored nutrition can have on our furry friends. We've witnessed transformations, heard heartwarming stories, and seen dogs regain their vitality and joy. It's a testament to the bond we share with our pets and the lengths we'll go to ensure their well-being.

But this journey doesn't end here. We invite you to continue exploring the world of allergy-friendly meals, experimenting with new recipes, and sharing your experiences with us. Your feedback is invaluable as it helps us refine our recipes and create an even better cookbook in the future.

If you've experienced success with our recipes, please share your story with us. Your triumphs inspire us, and they can inspire others who are on a similar journey with their dogs. If you faced challenges or have suggestions for improvement, we're eager to hear from you too. Your insights can help us make this cookbook even more effective.

Together, as a community of dog lovers and advocates for their well-being, we can continue to make a difference in the lives of our furry companions. We look forward to hearing from you, learning from you, and embarking on new culinary adventures together.

Thank you for choosing the Dog Food Cookbook for Food Allergies. Here's to a future filled with vibrant health, wagging tails, and the boundless joy of sharing meals with our cherished dogs.

BONUS: Homemade Allergy Test Guides.

GUIDE 1: AT-HOME ALLERGY TEST

Step 1: Preparation

- Gather necessary supplies, including hypoallergenic dog food, potential allergen sources, and a notebook to record observations.

Step 2: Elimination Diet

- Start with an elimination diet, feeding only hypoallergenic dog food for a minimum of eight weeks. Avoid all potential allergens.

Step 3: Monitor Symptoms

- Record any changes in your dog's condition during the elimination period. Note improvements or continued symptoms.

Step 4: Reintroduce Potential Allergens

- Gradually reintroduce one potential allergen at a time while closely monitoring your dog's reactions. Allow a minimum of one week between each allergen introduction.

Step 5: Record Reactions

- Document any allergic reactions, such as itching, gastrointestinal issues, or changes in behavior, when reintroducing specific allergens.

Step 6: Identify Allergens

- Compare your notes to pinpoint which allergens trigger reactions in your dog. This will help you identify and avoid problem ingredients.

GUIDE 2: FOOD TRIAL TEMPLATE

Step 1: Select Test Ingredients

- Choose a single novel protein source (e.g., venison or duck) and a single carbohydrate source (e.g., sweet potatoes or rice).

Step 2: Preparation

- Prepare a small batch of homemade dog food using the selected ingredients. Ensure it's free from all potential allergens.

Step 3: Monitor Symptoms

- Feed this homemade dog food exclusively for eight weeks, carefully observing your dog for any changes in health or behavior.

Step 4: Gradual Introductions

- After the trial period, you can gradually introduce one potential allergen at a time, following the same process as in Guide 1.

Step 5: Record Observations

- Maintain detailed records of your dog's reactions during the food trial, helping you identify any triggers.

These Homemade Allergy Test Guides are designed to assist you in identifying your dog's specific allergies and sensitivities. Remember that every dog is unique, and it may take time and patience to uncover the culprits behind your dog's allergies.

Made in the USA
Monee, IL
06 April 2024

78ab0eae-3240-47b1-934a-c4786f3b39b7R01